The Atrocity of Water

# The Atrocity of Water

Poetry

**Kirsten Hemmy**

Press 53
Winston-Salem

Press 53
PO Box 30314
Winston-Salem, NC 27130

First Edition

Copyright © 2010 by Kirsten Hemmy

A Tom Lombardo Poetry Selection

All rights reserved, including the right of reproduction in whole or in part in any form. For permission, contact author at editor@Press53.com, or at the address above.

Cover design by Kevin Morgan Watson

Cover photo, "Water Drop." Copyright © 2010 by Brandon C. Watson

Printed on acid-free paper

ISBN 978-1-935708-12-4

*This book is dedicated to the memory of
two great teachers and mentors,
Lucille Clifton and Herb Scott.*

# Acknowledgments

Grateful acknowledgment is made to the editors of the following journals in which these poems first appeared:

"Afterwards in Manoa," *Sonora Review*
"The Atrocity of Water," *Alaska Quarterly Review*
"Birthday Flowers," *Green Mountains Review*
"Collective," *CaKe Magazine*
"The Fact of the Matter," *Southern Humanities Review*
"Fragmentation," *Antioch Review*
"Kilauea Iki," *Chaminade Literary Review*
"My Grandfather Tells Me a Story About His Life," "Ruby,"
    *Bellingham Review*
"Sahara," *Broad River Review*

Many thanks to the North Carolina Humanities Council for their support & publication of a number of poems that appear here, through the Linda Flowers Literary Award.

Thanks also to those who've loved & supported these poems & my process: Kimberly Blaeser, Antoinette Brim, Marcel Brouwers, Arthur Camara, Karen Carcia, Colena Corbett, Jamie D'Agostino, Chris Davis, Amy DeJarlais, Gorgui Dieng, Kevin Dockerty, Nancy Eimers, Blas Falconer, Susan Firer, Joanne Gabbin, Bob Hicok, Damaris Hill, Eno Ikpe, Richard Katrovas, John Koethe, Yusef Komunyakaa, Debra Kim, Rachel Levine, Tom Lombardo, Beth Martinelli, CP Maze, Adela Najarro, Jason Olive, William Olsen, Hermine Pinson, Billy Reynolds, Metta Sama, Susan Schultz, Evie Shockley, Lupe Solis, Darren Vincent, Kevin Watson, Patricia Jabbeh Wesley, Cornel West, Jameka Whitten, Antoine Williams, Al Young, and Kyoko Yoshida.

# Contents

Introduction / xi

**Prologue**

Then / xv

# I

New at Things / 3
Dear Beyond / 4
Winter in the Carolinas / 5
Sacred Geometry / 6
*Kunoni* –To Progress (Slowly) / 7
*Hili Po* / 8
Sophisticated Hula / 10
Lament / 11
Sabbath / 12
Landscape in Two Parts / 13
*Ile de Goree*, On Visiting the Slave House / 15
A Part Of / 18
The Lost Hours / 19
Semantics of Rape / 20
Dear Gone / 21

# II

Deconstruction / 25
Sacred Geometry / 27
Last Night I Watched You Dance / 28
Confession in Three Parts / 29

Zen Love Poem / 31
Loss / 32
You & Me, Love: Some Thoughts on Relationships / 33
Birthday Flowers / 35
Sometimes / 36
*In Medias Res* / 37
Dangerous Love Poem / 38
The Atrocity of Water / 39
*Kilauea Iki*: Devastation Trail / 40

## III

Afterwards in Manoa / 43
Ruby / 45
My Grandfather Tells Me a Story About His Life / 46
Rainy Season / 47
Sacred Geometry / 48
Sahara / 49
In Niger / 50
Fragmentation / 51
The Fact of the Matter / 53
*Hawai'i Ne* / 55
Collective / 56
Mortal / 58
Anniversary / 60
Even in This Bad Year / 62
Elegy for Places I've Left / 63

## Introduction

Kevin Watson, publisher of Press 53, and I first came across poet Kirsten Hemmy while perusing the North Carolina Humanities Council's magazine *NC Conversations*. The issue contained 10 poems by the winner of the council's 2008 Linda Flowers Literary Award for Poetry—Ms. Hemmy. We fell in love with her poems on the spot—her events of language are simply breathtaking—and invited her to send a manuscript to Press 53.

Ms. Hemmy's poems resound with the wind, the water, and the paradox that is Hawaii—the isolated paradise.

Your gentle hands are the dance—the
story, too—& still tell men all they need
to know...
the distance of the past is like a ship encroaching
from the horizon, the infringing of the horizon itself.

   —from "Sophisticated Hula," page 10

Her poems delve into the sensitivities of race and color discovered as she emigrated from a place where nearly everyone was a racial polyglot to the American South, where even joining a church had racial implications.

House of people whose eyes do not meet.
White people. The reason I first joined
a black church. Black people…

In the South, I wonder. Am I an eyesore.
My brown skin not white. My light skin not dark.

>…I am an island
girl without water in sight…

> —from "Collective," p. 56

Like the oceans, this collection embraces the globe and all nations. Ms. Hemmy tells the stories of her extensive stays in Africa, once on a Fulbright in Senegal and another stint in Ghana and Nigeria, and visits to other Saharan nations. She is a sharp and poetic observer of her own horrifying experiences ("Semantics of Rape," p. 20) and those of others, both past ("*Ile de Gore*, On Visiting the Slave House," pp. 15) and present ("In Niger," p. 50).

She traces for us through her stories, images, and tropes a path to follow—if not to acceptance—to a deeper level of understanding. Perhaps she suggests that we cling to what Senegalese women searching for water each day carry with them as the Sahara spreads and wells dry up:

a formula to measure it all:
fear, rope, bucket, thirst, hope.

> —from "Sacred Geometry," p. 48

Ms. Hemmy has seen her share of the grittiness of the world, but she hasn't let the dark parts of the human soul disable her. She feels the world drop by drop and that becomes the energy source for her poetry. Then she illuminates the glistening of hope within our souls.

Tom Lombardo
Poetry Editor, Press 53

**Then**

We were one once, it's true.

You un-broke me, shard by

jagged shard, until my lightness

fell away, until it deepened

like the sky—& we breathed

the light, which we believed

couldn't remain without us.

I

## New at Things

History is also a body. Am I so small

in my apartment at night that nothing

notices my presence or absence.

In the ocean I once recognized touching

everything & nothing all at once.

Simulacrum. & here there are gunshots

that look like shooting stars, luminescent

in deep sea of—light that takes life,

men filching women on jogging trails

at dusk & I too am disappearing. No one

asks, do I know the story of the city yet.

The constellation of loneliness created

by ourselves. So many of us clambering

together, brushing sky, brushing skin to

sinew to skin. It's the same story all over

town: streams of people, tight spaces &

open sky. Everywhere, we are swimming.

## Dear Beyond

> *Happy the eyes that can close.*
> — Alan Paton, *Cry the Beloved Country*

Tell me if this is true: I want to know
what survives us, what's bequeathed

from mother to daughter, what's passed
across oceans & migrations & border

crossings of the soul & every imaginable
landscape. Some nights I dream of cities

rising brick by brick, cream colored &
pink, flesh-like & built on enslaved sweat,

fishermen cleaning silver kettles of pewter
fish, their eyes slab gray & forced open

by death, atrociously seeing & seeing &—
men bent close to the earth, arms like scythes,

mountains grizzled with pine trees, ash
trees swiped down for love of money, starved

boys, girls turned to ash, men & women made
into soap, people loved & hated beyond

reason, an ocean of memories—all mine
even in their hideous persistence, rolling in—

which slosh against my skull. I wake to
shadows I have been or will become:

flutter of leaf to ground, birds returning,
too early, to naked trees. Movement

in the corner of everywhere. What is there
unrepeatable, what cannot be handed down?

## Winter in the Carolinas

Some days
its lack pulls at me, the sense of missing
something I have come to know well
inside this lonely town, little world

its absence
palpable, shimmering. Silence.
Some evenings when quite alone
I walk in the dark, my mind in the faraway

& watch the sky
enjoy the distance of stars & galaxies
through a slow dull air,
the light like white brilliance, finding more time in time.

There is a symbiosis
in the weather, in the stars, in the blackness which envelops
like a lack or a glut. I battle myself, the night breeze so familiar
& yet also so foreign, untranslatable.

## Sacred Geometry

*It can't be told*, or *he might could
do it*—in fits & spurts I adjust idiotically,

idiomatically to the South. *Where I'm from*,
I take to saying, a preface to everything

that is articulable & so much beyond, until
one night I wake from a dream of the ocean

& I am sweating, then cold, still & alone.
What I can't fathom is the fathomless:

how we get from here to here, all the lonely
displaced placing themselves all over town.

The problem is solved for $x$ or $y$, but
the question comes from a book or a class

I'm unfamiliar with. & this I think is what wakes
me. All bodies, all the bodies fall at 9.8 meters per

second per second, something I can barely grasp as
I drift back to sleep. What keeps me: far off sounds

of water, innate sense of simple math, straight
lines bridging $a$ to $b$, past to now, dear to gone.

## *Kunoni* — To Progress (Slowly)

*Charlotte, NC, September 20, 2007*

Freedom is what you do
with what's been done

to you, someone once said.
Not tonight, not here

in the South. Or,
yes. The dusk falls into

the sky. Everything in
flux. You can feel it,

all stars & possibility.
The city, named

for a queen, always too busy
& too divided. Whites

here wore black to support
the kids in Jena, Louisiana,

but in their walk & their words
that distinction, the always *us*

& *them*-ing. The *deep* South.
As if it isn't here.

There is a saying:
the wave

can never be afraid of
the ocean. Or should not be.

## Hili Po

*for Cory Lanakila Carroll, in memoriam*

In our language is to wander in the dark. How
far it was to fall. Too far. Your voice is mine,

cousin. When you died I died. I have not yet awakened.
I never saw the light. I am always looking at fire.

It is exhausting & it is life. Sounds scare me
the way that silence does. I listen but don't hear.

I can't remember my childhood. A shrink tells me
it's because of the violence. I remember all of that.

Just nothing good. Certainly, there was something.
A boyfriend tells me I use my past against me, calls

me self-saboteur. I say I am a writer. I have to do
something with it. I write it down. He beds half

the city. I deserve it, I suppose. Perhaps this is humanity.
There is so much worse in the world. I've learned from you

& from our ancestors that we can endure many things, which
is not the same as immortality. But you must live on, even

now when you have stopped haunting me. I try to document
it all. I try to see it all, & to escape unscathed. I understand

the impossibility of escaping pain. I attempt to be strong, even
though each generation gets lighter & lighter still. I had fictive

friends until I was too old; in my back yard & neighborhood
I made up stories, built an imaginary city. We were: near

the ocean, of the water, a strong Polynesian people never
reduced to what those other characters, my mother &

father, had to become. Even they were never villains
in our city, just beaten & beaten & reduced to it: alcohol,

a poverty of spirit & self, a longing for something
that beats in the blood, that is foreign but also innate. This

is what I studied in school; they, the wretched of the earth.
My white classmates took notes while I thought of home.

With my imaginary friends, it was easy: we spoke our native
tongue, ruled ourselves with the love & compassion we deserved.

We were righteous, & in fact, we did get what was ours:
*Ho'oikaika*, we were gathering strength, preparing for the rest

of our lives. *Ha'ina mai kapuana.* Let the story be told. We are
nothing if not heartbreaking. You are nothing if not imagined.

## Sophisticated Hula

> *for* Halau Na Wahine O Hawai'i

Your gentle hands are the dance—

the story, too—& still tell men all they need

to know. It is a history, your story. In this way,

you are still a queen, even after it has been unfolded &

retold by pineapples, sugar, missionaries & the plantation

years. Your feet are still lithe & just the right step moves

your hips with power & seduction. Your hair is still

black. *Ehu* blonde strands catch in the sun's snare.

Even this suggests your history is complicated, the story

long & involved. Surely, you already know the dance

which tells this story, the wild patience of loosing hips,

feet & hands, the distance of the past like a ship encroaching

from the horizon, the infringing of the horizon itself.

# Lament

*after James Wright*

The wind is so cool here in the mountains;

It is an almost blue, the color of lungs

Before the sun rises. A cow calls

To the early morning stars; a rooster is restless

Somewhere down the road. Wind strokes

Wind chimes, a frivolous game, the push and pull

Required to make music. Riposte: the smooth

Whisper of morning birds, together in the dark

Hibiscus trees, just outside the window.

Silver swords swoon in the waning moonlight.

Soon, the sun will warm the world. The night always

Fails, & some mornings, this is the only sadness there is.

# Sabbath

> *from the black & white photograph, "Winter Scene,"*
> *Johnson C. Smith University, 1944.*

The day is thick & slow with ice. Quiet with
snow. Not peaceful—several wars going on.

Up in DC, today & every Sunday, 12 law students
from Howard meet at the People's Drug Store

to sit at the counter & not be served. Back
in Charlotte, the scene has been silenced by all

this snow. An occasional streetcar sludges up Trade
to Beatties Ford Road, past hedges & mistletoe

that flank these preeminent black ivory towers.
There is a clock tower amongst the austere buildings,

high above threadbare trees. In the heart of
the campus, the faith. Time heals; more than that,

it is a witness to it all. This picture is too quiet,
obfuscating. Magnolia trees that will grow and grow.

Snow. Chapter house. Line of stones. Not quite dusk,
another snowfall impregnating the sky. Smoke lifts from

each building's chimney. Inside, men arm themselves
with books & voices. The youngest feeds the fire.

The poets write their history—the long, the short,
the difficult minutes of night, Southern & vile.

## Landscape in Two Parts

*l'esclavage*—a child holds chains

there is a reservoir

somewhere

not

here—

the cramped & fetid

waiting rooms of

history

*

in a field

notebook

she records

the cotton, not

free labor

high profits

low overhead

but the way

she saved her son

from the same

hell

with the rusted

meat cleaver late

on a Sunday afternoon

## *Ile de Goree*, On Visiting the Slave House

I.

The ferry is a blast of diesel fumes. A few years back,
a boat like this sank & thousands drowned off the coast
of Senegal, bodies scorched by white heat, bloated

by death mere miles from sand & safety. It was our
September 11th, Janaba says. I am squeezed, face twisted
& limbs cleaving; we are all touching each other.

So many bodies in the boat: the rules for crossing
the Atlantic were made by someone who looked like
me. There are no rules. I hold my breath.

II.

The island itself is beautiful. Colonial, pastels
& sand. Having been the only *toubab*, white
foreigner, on the boat, at the dock I am mobbed

by people who want me to help, be of use
this time, come to shops, see henna fabrics, buy
earthen jewels. Between us stand so many

silences of the world. When I say I am here to see
the house what I mean is no thank you, I would love
to but can't, what won't we do to each other?

III.

The house is pink & faded. We go downstairs first.
Janaba tells me she didn't learn enough about slavery
as a child. We are the same age. There are chambers

downstairs, no windows at all in some rooms, tiniest
slats in concrete in others, like I've seen in forts.
These are not for guns or rifles but the simplest self-

defense of breathing, of looking at the ocean's churn. I
walk to the door of no return, named so for what it
really was. For years the waters grew shark-infested

after recognition crept in, a cloud: getting on that ship
meant something less comprehensible than death or even
living. People, their bodies, jumped in throngs.

I stand in the women's dungeon for a long time.

In the men's room are wall scars, monuments
to shoulder blades rubbing for lack of space
& the fact that nothing can compare to hurt

inflicted on people by other people. Darkness
downstairs resonates against the walls, wet
& cold: throat & heart of stone. The souls

are everywhere & fathomless. I am stunned
by the acidic light upstairs. It is daylight,
astonishing, stinging. The staircase is

grand, a ballroom, regal, arched & sloping.
Lonely & exquisite. I count each stair—
15 steps is all the separation. Upstairs,

I cannot look at the jewelry, the wine & art,
labyrinth of wealth & infinite distances. I
keep my head down, notice the warped wood

of the floorboards, how they don't always
line up, good & evil, shadow cleaving to light.
On my knees, I see bodies walking in the dungeon.

IV.

Afterwards Janaba & I meet outside. Not
talking, we stare at the ocean, said to have
a riptide known to pull people out to sea

in the blink of a life. Beauty frightens
with possibility, its desire & want. We stand
close together & our skin touches, my arm

brushing hers, a softness. There is no wind
& the sun is scorching, yet we feel it, a shudder—
the indifference of water, the stopless renewal.

## A Part Of

One evening just afterwards, I walk

down the road after twilight until

the light is gone & my body is no more

than a part of the darkness. I could easily have

flinched or run, but I wanted to own it, I suppose:

the words late in coming to the lips, the lips themselves.

## The Lost Hours

Even when I have dismissed them all—
the barber, the trick on the corner,

the man who shows up in my dreams.
What is this night—the darkness, the moon,

the streetlights giving way to the fog
that encroaches like a beast. I run &

I hear it all: the gun blast, jazz, the man
kicking his woman in her ribs, a soft harp,

until she falls to the street & pleads, a trumpet
from someone's bedroom window. I have

kept the lost hours like my mother kept
what she could—our hair, our teeth,

the things we lost in our childhoods.
No one ever told us that we might need

to keep hold of so much that gives way
to time: my mother's memory, my father,

holidays & birthdays & the words *I love you*
& cakes & even the memory of these things.

I have kept the lost hours, those days I lived
in Ghana, where the child slept on the street,

the boy who followed me until we both got
lost. Even my rapist, I keep him, it, the night—

I could tell you what the darkness looked like &
the sweet, sweet shape of the moon. The scent

of plantains & hibiscus. I have kept the lost
hours, trying to do what, I don't know.

## Semantics of Rape

I think I get stuck
on *almost*, its taste sharp & sticking

in my throat, the same as *knife*, as *is*.
It is true after all, that you change

your words & form follows. Memory is
a frightening thing, so same as real, & it is

what gets people lost & found: I wake
some nights, my mouth a perfect circle, choking

on you, the fear as real as taste, as fighting
the impulse to either kill you or give in.

## Dear Gone

A group of men stands in my path.
The sound of night winds, hissing past

arms & legs. From a distance I can't
make out whether they are talking,

praying or plotting. There are soldiers
in their voices. Single laugh. Sinister.

Figment. Maybe. I reach my hand
to my face, a nervous gesture, basest

instinct. I live behind it, feeling myself
flinch at every step. I try to memorize

the faces & instead find myself creating
figments of stories, fragments, fiction.

Before, walking at night was like being
free. A moment of almost, of the kind

of peace reserved for darkness & stars.
But now a gesture grazes the threat,

constricting with possibility. I see
the shadows of rapists everywhere.

Their eyes, otherworldly & knowing.
Every eye is the same. It wants & wants

& —. I'll never know. I know them all.
I want to *be* again. The going back, so slow.

I want to kill all men, piece by piece, take
them in my hands, blow their shards into

the stars, put them at peace with the world. But
this isn't hate. This is fight. Flight. Unconstraint.

II

## Deconstruction

It is a river. It is a waterfall.

Her hair caressing.

Cascade.

Her neck.

The getting lost as to beginning & end.

Whose skin. Where.

Stream.

Rivers in her hands.

An etching into granite.

Skyline at dawn.

Objects splicing late afternoon.

A lightness so bright.

Darkness the same.

Surfaces & edges. Patterns &.

Sometimes symmetry.

Cartesian dream.

Inner quest a landscape, still.

Geometry of the soul & deeper.

Testimony of.

The smooth lip on a ceramic mug.

Curve of hip—her body a cello.

Concentric.

Consenting.

Harp of ribs.

Fingers trace.

A kind of longing.

Impermanence.

Rise & fall of breath.

Music. Even softer.

## Sacred Geometry

Night out. I hold
my breath like lovers
hold one another. Outside

it is moonlit, the skies all
city & show. Floodlight
of pattern, possibility.

Inside, there is a meeting.
It is a union much like
anything which begins

from nothing, which is
everything. Spiral of
disparate moving together.

The pianist, his feet
dancing on stage despite
the austere reserve of

the philharmonic. Gospel
choir in back, a rainbow
in black & white, beaming

moon of silk, dazzling
voices that hurt the soul
with pain & sweetness both.

## Last Night I Watched You Dance

*for Promise Ansah*

For hours, your body beautiful,
moving like light across the godwall.

My pulse was the fifth drum, sharp
& talking in thunder. I became

the rhythm, but the rhythm was
my blood. I made a wish with every step:

you a part of me, your name
something I could swallow whole,

your dancing the sound of
drums left after the music ends.

## Confession in Three Parts

1. *"But you crushed us and made us a haunt for jackals and covered us over with deep darkness." (Psalm 44:19)*

This numbness is in me, no
*is* me—even though my hair &
skin is damp with after, even after
holy water & the metaphorical body
& blood, even as I notice the women
crying & the preacher pleading, sending
his hands into our hearts, which stay
clenched, even as they will to open.


2. *"Dark am I, yet lovely….";  "How beautiful you are…. Oh, how beautiful! Your eyes are doves." (Song of Songs 5, 15)*

Women with wide hips sway
on either side of me: the music is
moving, & the preacher's message
that we, the marginalized, can come
through the door. All seekers are
welcome here. Even you, the beautiful
who, tragically, are far too shattered
to see what it is you're looking at.

3. *"Lift up your skirts, bare your legs, and wade through the streams. Your nakedness will be exposed…."* (Isaiah 47:2-3)

Desire has sealed my mouth.
I know my story all too well
& yet I dance this silhouette between
worlds, afraid to cross the river, even
at night. This barge of a heart is
a ballroom's dazzle & I stay adrift,
floating from one side of the bank to
the other. I sleep with men because
they desire me, I love women because
it is the only way I know how.

## Zen Love Poem

Once again I become nothing, so that even then,

we are one. Our words across the bed, reaching

into the damp night sky, taking shape beyond

the splatter of stars, light gone by the time it reaches us.

## Loss

Across the room, the man. Whom I never intended
to love. We are altogether wrong. He is. I am. The path.

But. In our occasioned embrace, what is nearly
a voice, or the sting of the ocean on skin, afternoon

light slipping into a long-dark room, drench of fall moon
into each corner. Intent pull of moon against ocean tide,

light into dark into——. Playfulness has begotten something real.
This something frightens; it has not been called for. We strain

to undo it. The distance, a lone lean dog, hurries away. Despite
sometimes miserable efforts, we wake to find its absence as

a presence. Its face fades; eventually, we will even forget its name.

## You & Me, Love: Some Thoughts on Relationships

> *The transformative power of love is not fully embraced in our society because we often wrongly believe that torment and anguish are our "natural" condition.*
> — bell hooks

Old male idea of honor, color of rust, a kind of alchemy,

color of late summer sky just before dark. Implied:

truth. Lying done with words & with silence, maybe not

planned or invented—real talk. Fear. Fear. Fear of

losing control, that little hummingbird flutter

in an abdomen, dancing up into the throat. By now

you cannot even desire a relationship without

manipulation, a kind of melody like the sound of

home, childhood hook you never fully get out of

your head. Vulnerability to another = loss of control.

What we had: quantum love, physics of, spotlight

I shined into an abyss. Something unnamed within:

dim stars, fear of that being all the light there is.

Fear you are destined to remain powerless. In that

struggle to survive you learned lies, learned to love

their taste, sweet & easy like liquor, filling the dark

core, drowning that fear that your truths are not

good enough, fear of falling, fear of the page, blank as

the life you believe you have lived up to this moment.

## Birthday Flowers

She knew she'd killed them, & after only two months. She did it
on purpose, not in the beginning, but finally, eventually. They were red
and gold, a gift from someone who loved her, & she had been

doing so well for them. It was a sunny day, after so much fall
drear—warm, & she decided they could use the sunshine,
the deck, the outside. Placed them benignly between the slats

of sun, watched their yellow faces open, turn to face
the light. Later, in the cold bleak of mid-afternoon she turned on
the heat, made tea, & watched them through the window.

The green leaves on the stems shivered & shrank, the flowers hung
their yellowed heads. She watched the water in the holding dish, tried
to determine if its stillness meant ice. She listened to the birds, far-off

calls of geese. She listened to Mozart. She puttered inside. Too cold
for a run. The clouds swallowed the sun; the night ingested the day.
& she looked out into the dank, liked how she could apprehend

their outline, absurd & sacrosanct, the way that they were still
there. Their red & gold resilience, their resolve, was something
unconstrained—she thought this later, as she swept

her house clean. It was improbable, something like begetting,
like what the sun gives the world after cold autumn night, after black
hours away, & the only way to see is to compare darknesses.

## Sometimes

All the tragedies of the world are

a silence. The stillness is not love.

I want to ask. I hear it on the wires,

rustling in the trees, along a breeze

that sometimes creeps across our city.

What made me not enough—this is

the sheen of the moon, the heaviness of

the stars in the sky. The world is a liar—.

Did you? There was beauty, surely. To finish

the question is to understand what it is to be a fool.

## In Medias Res

*for CP Maze, the Concrete Generation Slam Poets, Charlotte, NC*

The world has put its hands all over us, & we have both learned to yield to this kind of intimacy. We've learned what to do with silence, with now & with gone & with prayer. But here our paths have crossed, our bodies dream-heated & our minds curious. Still, you stay. & come closer. You too have told me the world is topside down or outside in, that for us to sleep at all would be to close our eyes inside a bullet—cheek to cheek, in public anonymity—to feel the utter loneliness that comes from a reckless closeness, the after that follows abandonment of reason. Free spirits believe in providence, in chance, in the accidental beauty of rain at midnight, the yellow certainty of late afternoon. The air between us an idea, nothing but the rhythm of breath. Everything held this moment in place—I drew you in my mind as you are, hoping to recreate you here, now, without distractions of the ghosts inside us, the brokenness of the body. The sky is bright with dusk & I have been watching my shadow fold in on itself, without words, devolving into a deeper shade of darkness until it disappears. You asked why we write, what makes a poet. Here. I am showing you. This darkness is the body of our words:we write to understand we're not alone in it—even though it is ours to do alone.

## Dangerous Love Poem

Wet bright moss under & over the stream. Against.
The stream itself, cold, mountainous, dark like

the mountains themselves. How from a distance
they'd seemed more like hills, less cragged &

risky. Rain from fog, its caress sharp, almost:
cool on my warm cheek like an accidental slap.

The loosing of the hands, the body limber &
bending to plunge rushing waters. Oh, the sound

of water on rock, friction of two improbable bodies
meeting, movement of, whisper-gurgle of one &

one touching the other. The noise, a kind of music.
Bodies together—the breaking open of one against

itself or the other, the getting lost as to which is
which. Lightness crafted within harshest landscape.

Green, mere life, surviving nearly everywhere.
Water-beaded heaviness of ferns. The unfurling.

## The Atrocity of Water

Water has a beautiful smell in certain places. Or
it is the full, wet air, which smells of water. As I write

this we are traveling by cab to my cousins' house
in Pearl City on the island of O'ahu. We drive over

a bridge that was bombed. We drive past the military
base where the water is so clear—a violent violet that

exposes the dialectics of war. The bridge we travel
spans a great historical distance: today, the hellish orange

halos of fire are swallowed by water; they've stopped
bombing the island of Kaho'olawe. The lesson is

that you can own everything. The lesson is that we can
stand for anything, even water. Our cab driver is impressed

that my cousin teaches at Keio University ("it is the Harvard
of Japan"), & using his broken pidgin tries to engage us

in a conversation about Heidegger's "Question
Concerning Technology." But I am thinking about water—

all the oceans that bring us together, that separate
with a nihilism that eats the oxygen from the water,

from the skies, leaving blue the color of guns, of corpse.
Water can be deep & voiceless. We can need it.

We are almost over the bridge now.

## *Kilauea Iki:* Devastation Trail

On cloudy nights after surf-drenched days
the soft scorch of *pahoehoe*, lava drifting,

on fire, to the sea—slow black moans of
resignation as Yamaguchi's Kalapana Store,

schools & homes give way to the supple blanket.
So much will endure:

the store's decrepit neon sign, a stillness,
the heaviness of someone's memories.

Years later, nothing will bay at the moon
from this earth except the darkness.

A woman will hear emptiness like whispers
as she wanders the hardened mountainside,

considering the barren luridness,
the lies of fire, smoldering.

III

## Afterwards in Manoa

*for Jen*

The first evening after your death, it is important
for me to know that it is not a prank—I am swimming
at the university pool, the one where we'd exhausted our youth—

a man, practically all skin, looks at me & says "I'm sorry"
to the gray slab of cement at his feet; our coach, one time object
of sexual possibility pulls me into his office, shuts

the heavy blue door, & I think that it's a surprise,
a party for me, some ridiculous celebration
under the guise of death. Where have I been

that I haven't heard the news? He is trying to protect
me; his hand is a soft white scorpion against my thigh.
This moment has everything to do with your life.

I am sitting on the plaid couch with my eyes closed.
*She wasn't in pain,* he says, & *it wasn't her fault.* I cannot
open my eyes—this is not the way we imagined our intimate

instants with this man. I suspect it was different for you & him—
I can see that he is holding himself together for this
miserable moment under fluorescent light. He is brittle & essential

& I think, *be careful.* I ask him to come outside
with me. There are others there— absurd, men & women
waiting, watching in their swimsuits. The place is lit up

like a ballpark, but when we walk to the north
end of the complex, we can see the blue mountains
pushed up against the sky. We lean against the artificial

blue of the fence, bask in the chemical light
of the pool. We are silent, & our skin touches
in a way that makes me wonder if the whole world

comprises this very second. There is an empty
shiver: my eyes are open. There is no surprise—
the world is blue; the moment of death, instant.

# Ruby

My Australian grandmother only calls when this mood strikes
her, hot & stifling as the outback sun. It's a mixed blessing:

I know she's okay, but I can also hear the trouble in her
voice. Tonight she tells me: the moon is deep, the sky

blue-black, the world shaping itself like an exquisite opal,
flickering with late night, with summer, with dust-dirt,

stained feet, & the distance of the world between us. She
tells me it's torrid there, completely without wind, & there's

no relief except the ocean. She can't swim; & besides,
the salt isn't good for her hair, which she's dyed again

with henna—opulent red, night club dress of youth red,
a balloon drifting over goldenrod meadow red, coral

in the tide-pool red, umbrella held out to catch the rain
long ago red, sweet red, impossible red, long ago red.

## My Grandfather Tells Me a Story About His Life

Ruby dyed her hair red until the last few years
when she couldn't remember to do it, he says,

tentative & soft, as not to startle my own
memories of my grandmother. But at the end,

he continues, perhaps the mind only remembers
itself as it wants, anyway: she at her most exquisite

red-headed self. The mind releases the body
from its humanness, this marvelous weight,

at some point—beauty is, time flies as it never
moves, the larger landscape becoming the soul.

At night, he says, I sleep with it all—
we drive along the countryside, red earth, red

dirt, opal skies, broken hills, passing by all
the things we've loved in this world.

# Rainy Season

Grand Dakar: the road in front
of the house, *Rue X*, is flooded again

& for a third time this week I wade
through water which is knee or thigh

deep & sharp with glass & stones, thick
& mute with human & other sewage. I cut

a sandal on rubble & step hip high into
a pothole. I think for a moment to find

a cab in this river of people, cars & animals
scurrying. But the rain has its way with me, too,

& anyway it is faster to walk. Everything
has slowed down: for once I am unafraid

of cars & cross the street that leads
to market, careful only of waste floating past.

People are happy for the idea of rain, blizzard
of relief for the crops, & catch water in bowls

for drinking, cooking & bathing. White
laundry hangs slack on a line between

watery buildings, souls are wet with hope
& possibility: there is something about

feeling the world drop by drop, seeing it
accumulate in all its true grit & glisten.

## Sacred Geometry

I figure every day into
lightness of sand, or darkness

of people, night without
city of dust, of stars, of

cosmic & human drift. Hours
let go of letting go, wells

dry but the certainty of water
is somewhere. I walk, spend

all day searching with women—
dry skies, afternoon mirages

a formula to measure it all:
fear, rope, bucket, thirst, hope.

## Sahara

Women need water & wells,
spend all day wandering barren

landscapes looking for either.
Buckets on heads & carried

on high, hoping. The Peace
Corps built a top notch well

in Ndiayene but it's empty
for lack of rain. This

the women learn at a day's
cost—thirst & dirt, hunger &

thirst. This place where the desert is
migrating in, uninvited. It's called

desertification, a mouthful
but painful to swallow, dry,

this creeping across, this
cleaving to, this changing of

everything, this relentless
& rootless, enduring drift.

## In Niger

Even after

visiting the camps

where we

do nothing but watch

men die &

women & children die

even faster,

Eno believes

that I am

starving. The burning

in my stomach

isn't so much

from hunger

as from

gluttony,

whose language

I finally

understand

is my

mother tongue.

# Fragmentation

I befriend a boy in Senegal who can
recite the Qu'ran three times—all

the way through—by the time he is
eight. He is a gift to the world, truly,

goes to private school even though
his parents can't pay the fees. I meet

his teachers, see their eyes, lonely &
proud. For all children in training,

the first lessons are prayers. These
are the foundation & must

be perfectly memorized if there is
any hope at all. It is through prayer

that the Imam, leader which this
boy will someday be, sends strength

& power to the masses. The words
have been written down over & over

again: the boy takes me to the library
of a prophet who spent his life

transcribing the Qu'ran. There
is nothing in the library but a thousand

books in his handwriting & the words
of the sacred. There must be a hunger

in such rhythms for them to have
survived it all: holy wars, famine,

disbelievers. I try to speak to the boy
in Arabic, which he doesn't understand.

I recite the only poems I know in French,
some Rimbaud, Baudelaire, & Mallarme.

These men are landmarks of failure,
of modernity: one's livelihood

ends in aphasia, the others abandon
their work, overcome by the notion

of the world's fragmentation. This is
something I'm not sure I can translate,

not sure this boy would understand. We
stand in silence, feeling the graves of those

around us, all the nameless lives less
somehow than ours. I wonder what will

become of this boy, all the places he
will travel in dream & through prayer.

He smiles, touches his hand to mine.
I can only speak to you in broken

things, I say, but don't tell him how
something of me longs to be shut.

The world is a beautiful place, he
says, almost a Paradise. The Qu'ran

says the world suffers, whispers
the boy, but I'll never know how.

# The Fact of the Matter

*for A.*

The way the ocean is a fact, & also
the way one can love it, a pure thing, true:

the girl's teeth, what we both noticed, white
like glass beads against fleshy pink mouth against

deep brown skin. In retrospect we might say
her dress was beautiful, but whether this is true

is arguable, is only memory: it was *kente*, but
not real, not woven from the loom; rather, fake

*kente*, batik or waxcloth, shining & ostentatious
in the sun's harsh glower. People talk about hard

facts, the way what's true sometime surprises
by its mere realness. What surprised us the most?

There was so much we carefully sidestepped later:
the girl, her smile, the heat like a light from

her body, running to cross the street. Midday
traffic, our holding our collective breath, the space

we shared & the shiver that happened when our heated
skin touched in that instant just after. The fact of

the matter for us, all humans: suffering. For the girl,
we'll never know. The car striking like midday

sun, the metal of afternoon, the everywhere
pebbles & shards of glass. Her body a body

like any other. Breakable. The ocean just beyond her,
bending like the body that it is, beneath the weight of

the sky & the whole world. All the silence of bodies
after they come to rest by choice or involuntarily.

The edge of fact, of: still life, still life, seizure into
death, the final breath, a smile. Fact: her body hit

the ground with such a force that neither us of could
forget that sound. & yet, we crossed that road minutes

later, further down, recollecting death as well as life.
Bodies groping in the dark are bodies like any others,

too. & your smile, your teeth, their whiteness like lovely
& familiar glass against your lips, your skin. This is true.

## Hawai'i Ne

Steel drums & rhythm—your pulse into
mine. Thighs. Brown eyes. Small, small

lies. *How about—?—Yes, there.* The story
line is also the horizon, the sun's departure

a green flash plunging into sea. Bodies
no longer islands. Our voices the same.

Whisper. Pidgin. Toes on the nose, ocean
beneath. Veins hard, branches spreading,

flowers, arms, legs. Rivers. Our breath is
water, tropical skies. Mangoes. Music like

tin roofs, rain, the quiet that comes. Surge of surf
in the distance, crashing into sand, again, again, again.

## Collective

> *If art is our only resistance, what does that make us?*
> —Adrienne Rich

House of people whose eyes do not meet.
White people. The reason I first joined
a black church. Black people.

My new family is used to accepting pain &
wearing it gently, & therefore they take me in,
put me on. Black is beautiful but I am too almost,

imperfectly shaped. A mismatch. Question
to my parents: how could you. Not following
the rule of law is who I am. Even when the law begs

questions it's still there to be followed.
In the South, I wonder. Am I an eyesore.
My brown skin not white. My light skin not dark.

Simplest blueprints of displacement: I dream
of the ocean, become a cliché, buy ocean-scented
everything. Blue becomes me, blue becomes

the symbol for all that has lost me.
What is to be done? Do I stay or can I go.
Tired & redundant I am. That was them

not me. I am an island
girl without water in sight. The imagination creates
mirage after mirage. The painting is on the wall. Where

is all that's yet to be written. Isolation begins
like death—the moment is almost
an instant. When did it all begin. More

than a question: what wrests beyond, where
is collective, is shared, is memory. Long ago
a boy of rage compelled by loss & love &

distance's song slew his brother.
His punishment: banishment & more distance,
a long lifetime of wandering barren lands.

## Mortal

There is the taboo of almost.
Would it be wrong to say

I am in love with my pastor.
We have eroticized our intellects,

made love madly in the slack swell
of poetry, our earnest souls

falling into philosophical arguments,
existential proximity of—.

Not knowing what to do
with that plentitude of loneliness

that comes from meeting someone
with whom you could derail

your whole, put-together life.
The mere thought of it.

This might be the very last
love affair there can be.

Would Freud call this
the oceanic effect, that longing

for my brother who is also
in many ways a father, & is

in actuality to family & flock.
There is, of course, the wife,

which is how this all began,
her hating me & me noticing;

his admission that she does
because, well, *it could happen.*

When I said it would never,
*I'm not that kind,* he said

he'd learned not to lean
on his own understanding, that

there remained a certain
relationship in our desire

to craft beauty with words.
We talked later over wine

about the ragged Self,
the inevitability of the fall.

How human of us, that
Pygmalion instinct, longing for

a lover the same as the self,
but different. Where space

should not exist either, we are
charmed by each other again & again.

# Anniversary

*after Lucille Clifton's "sorrows"*

Long past midnight, unseasonably warm.
A slow fog gets caught, catches

building edges & alleys, the street. I
drive the long way home, past the old

place on Everett, turning at the last
moment down that starlit stretch of

poverty, shotgun houses & lawn ornaments,
bullet-riddled street signs, trash at road's edge.

In the neighboring lot, same rusted couch
& mattress too, clothes & food & refuse, signs

of vagrants passing through, numb shadows
& light. It's been a year—blue skies & blue days,

blues of the body, my body trudging through
space & time, relearning what it is to be linear

& present. My own blood has spilled
a dozen times & for that I am thankful. I do not

hate him, I assure myself, not even his broken
heart. Comforts now privilege & this street,

all silent & barren, looks different. I stop
at the driveway, where I learned fear. (A small

country we made, a house but not a home.)
I'm alone but it's not the same. Even the spectrum

of dark has changed. Inside the house, who knows
what might remain. Who would believe even

our sorrows might be beautiful. Perhaps somewhere
an echo of love, even if it is only a single voice.

## Even in This Bad Year

the sun in summer makes the sky big,
blue, & clear. It's 95° today here in Atlanta

& there in Minnesota at the clinic
where my father lies dying, alone,

from brain cancer. It never seems fair:
too healthy, too young, too bright, devout too.

How hard it is, we say—just when we adjust
to the striking sun, its unrelenting rays, we grow

cold in the shade. Very soon it will be the end
of a beautiful summer. It will rain. We will

resort to speaking of such things. The sky
will gray, full of evening & of end.

## Elegy for Places I've Left

What gets remembered: the prodigal son, Joseph's dream,
loosened fist of the tree, magnolia blossoms strewn along
the river bank, a white trail leading to its end. The slowing

of the pulse at the Japanese garden, heart all twisted at first
like bonsai, later soft & careless as *honu* lounging in pond.
Late afternoon, sneaking in, the light slanting & certain,

all glorious like the sweet hymning of a spiritual, the sound
the ocean still makes in ears long after leaving the ocean.
The taste of salt which also remains on the lips & skin, white

like snow. Blue-black skies during a sluggish snow in the heart
of chill, middle of night. The urge to open the mouth, let
flakes catch on the tongue, shiver the eyelashes & nose.

The art of distance and of boundaries. The hard
look of the moon some nights, & in winter's
frigid slow motion, the sly pleasure of staring back.

KIRSTEN HEMMY is the Chair of Interdisciplinary Studies, Philosophy, and Religion at Johnson C. Smith University, Charlotte, North Carolina. She is also a member of the Southern Humanities Council executive board and the director of the Mosaic Literary Center of Charlotte, a nonprofit organization dedicated to the discovery, cultivation, and preservation of contemporary literature and the arts in underserved communities. She received her M.A. in Literary Studies from the University of Wisconsin at Milwaukee and her Ph.D. in Creative Writing from Western Michigan University. As a Fulbright Scholar in 2003, she studied politics and poetry in Senegal. Hemmy has also studied in Ghana and is currently completing a book on Emma Brown, an Ibibio freedom fighter and political activist in Nigeria. Hemmy's poetry has appeared in *Sonora Review*, *Alaska Quarterly Review*, *Spoon River Poetry Review*, *Green Mountains Review*, *Callyx*, *Cake Magazine*, *Midwest Poetry Review*, *Lake Effect*, *Bellingham Review*, *Southern Humanities Review*, *Cream City Review*, *Smartish Pace*, *Antioch Review*, and elsewhere. She was the 2008 recipient of the Linda Flowers Literary Award, has received the Academy of American Poets Award, and has published interviews with poets such as Yusef Komunyakaa and Ralph Angel.

Cover Artist **BRANDON C. WATSON** enjoys finding that special shot or moment through photography. "The key," he says, "is the endless search for form, compelling subjects, patterns, and faces within the frame."

Specializing in macro photography, cityscapes and nature, Brandon has become an acclaimed photographer and digital artist.

Please check out his portfolio at brandonwatson.daportfolio.com

www.ingramcontent.com/pod-product-compliance
Lightning Source LLC
Chambersburg PA
CBHW051711040426
42446CB00008B/835